HORN

101 BROADWAY SONGS

Note: The keys in this book do not match the other wind instruments.

Available for
FLUTE, CLARINET, ALTO SAX, TENOR SAX, TRUMPET,
HORN, TROMBONE, VIOLIN, VIOLA, CELLO

ISBN 978-1-4950-5251-4

Hal•Leonard®
CORPORATION

7777 W. BLUEMOUND RD. P.O. BOX 13819 MILWAUKEE, WI 53213

Visit Hal Leonard Online at
www.halleonard.com

CONTENTS

ALL I ASK OF YOU

from THE PHANTOM OF THE OPERA

HORN

Music by ANDREW LLOYD WEBBER
Lyrics by CHARLES HART
Additional Lyrics by RICHARD STILGOE

ANY DREAM WILL DO

from JOSEPH AND THE AMAZING TECHNICOLOR® DREAMCOAT

Horn

Music by ANDREW LLOYD WEBBER
Lyrics by TIM RICE

ANYTHING YOU CAN DO

from the Stage Production ANNIE GET YOUR GUN

HORN

Words and Music by
IRVING BERLIN

AS IF WE NEVER SAID GOODBYE

from SUNSET BOULEVARD

Horn

Music by ANDREW LLOYD WEBBER
Lyrics by DON BLACK and CHRISTOPHER HAMPTON,
with contributions by AMY POWERS

AS LONG AS HE NEEDS ME

from the Broadway Musical OLIVER!

Horn

Words and Music by
LIONEL BART

BALI HA'I
from SOUTH PACIFIC

HORN

Lyrics by OSCAR HAMMERSTEIN II
Music by RICHARD RODGERS

BAUBLES, BANGLES AND BEADS

from KISMET

Horn

Words and Music by ROBERT WRIGHT
and GEORGE FORREST
(Music Based on Themes of A. BORODIN)

Moderately

BROTHERHOOD OF MAN

from HOW TO SUCCEED IN BUSINESS WITHOUT REALLY TRYING

Horn

By FRANK LOESSER

CABARET
from the Musical CABARET

HORN

Words by FRED EBB
Music by JOHN KANDER

CAN'T TAKE MY EYES OFF OF YOU

featured in JERSEY BOYS

Horn

Words and Music by BOB CREWE
and BOB GAUDIO

CIRCLE OF LIFE

Disney Presents THE LION KING: THE BROADWAY MUSICAL

HORN

Music by ELTON JOHN
Lyrics by TIM RICE

Moderately, with an African beat

CLIMB EV'RY MOUNTAIN

from THE SOUND OF MUSIC

Horn

Lyrics by OSCAR HAMMERSTEIN II
Music by RICHARD RODGERS

Majestically

CLOSE EVERY DOOR

from JOSEPH AND THE AMAZING TECHNICOLOR® DREAMCOAT

HORN

Music by ANDREW LLOYD WEBBER
Lyrics by TIM RICE

Moderately, expressively

DANCING QUEEN

from MAMMA MIA!

Horn

Words and Music by BENNY ANDERSSON,
BJÖRN ULVAEUS and STIG ANDERSON

DEFYING GRAVITY

from the Broadway Musical WICKED

HORN

Music and Lyrics by
STEPHEN SCHWARTZ

DO-RE-MI
from THE SOUND OF MUSIC

HORN

Lyrics by OSCAR HAMMERSTEIN II
Music by RICHARD RODGERS

Lively

DO YOU HEAR THE PEOPLE SING?

from LES MISÉRABLES

Horn

Music by CLAUDE-MICHEL SCHÖNBERG
Lyrics by ALAIN BOUBLIL, JEAN-MARC NATEL
and HERBERT KRETZMER

DON'T CRY FOR ME ARGENTINA

from EVITA

Horn

Words by TIM RICE
Music by ANDREW LLOYD WEBBER

EASTER PARADE

from AS THOUSANDS CHEER

HORN

Words and Music by
IRVING BERLIN

EDELWEISS
from THE SOUND OF MUSIC

HORN

Lyrics by OSCAR HAMMERSTEIN II
Music by RICHARD RODGERS

Slowly, with expression

EVERYTHING'S ALRIGHT

from JESUS CHRIST SUPERSTAR

Horn

Words by TIM RICE
Music by ANDREW LLOYD WEBBER

A FOGGY DAY (IN LONDON TOWN)

from A DAMSEL IN DISTRESS

Horn

Music and Lyrics by GEORGE GERSHWIN
and IRA GERSHWIN

GETTING TO KNOW YOU

from THE KING AND I

Horn

Lyrics by OSCAR HAMMERSTEIN II
Music by RICHARD RODGERS

FRIEND LIKE ME
(Stageplay Version)
from the Walt Disney Stageplay ALADDIN

Horn

Music by ALAN MENKEN
Lyrics by HOWARD ASHMAN
and STEPHEN SCHWARTZ

GUYS AND DOLLS

from GUYS AND DOLLS

HORN

By FRANK LOESSER

HELLO, DOLLY!

from HELLO, DOLLY!

Horn

Music and Lyric by
JERRY HERMAN

HOME

from Walt Disney's BEAUTY AND THE BEAST: THE BROADWAY MUSICAL

Horn

Music by ALAN MENKEN
Lyrics by TIM RICE

HOW ARE THINGS IN GLOCCA MORRA

from FINIAN'S RAINBOW

Horn

Words by E.Y. "YIP" HARBURG
Music by BURTON LANE

I BELIEVE IN YOU
from HOW TO SUCCEED IN BUSINESS WITHOUT REALLY TRYING

HORN

By FRANK LOESSER

I DON'T KNOW HOW TO LOVE HIM

from JESUS CHRIST SUPERSTAR

Horn

Words by TIM RICE
Music by ANDREW LLOYD WEBBER

Slowly, expressively

I DREAMED A DREAM

from LES MISÉRABLES

Horn

Music by CLAUDE-MICHEL SCHÖNBERG
Lyrics by ALAIN BOUBLIL, JEAN-MARC NATEL
and HERBERT KRETZMER

I GOT PLENTY O' NUTTIN'

from PORGY AND BESS ®

Horn

Music and Lyrics by GEORGE GERSHWIN,
DuBOSE and DORTHY HEYWARD
and IRA GERSHWIN

I WHISTLE A HAPPY TUNE

from THE KING AND I

Horn

Lyrics by OSCAR HAMMERSTEIN II
Music by RICHARD RODGERS

I'VE NEVER BEEN IN LOVE BEFORE

from GUYS AND DOLLS

Horn

By FRANK LOESSER

IF I LOVED YOU
from CAROUSEL

Horn

Lyrics by OSCAR HAMMERSTEIN II
Music by RICHARD RODGERS

IF I WERE A BELL

from GUYS AND DOLLS

Horn

By FRANK LOESSER

IF I WERE A RICH MAN

from the Musical FIDDLER ON THE ROOF

Horn

Words by SHELDON HARNICK
Music by JERRY BOCK

THE IMPOSSIBLE DREAM
(The Quest)
from MAN OF LA MANCHA

Horn

Lyric by JOE DARION
Music by MITCH LEIGH

IT AIN'T NECESSARILY SO

from PORGY AND BESS®

Horn

Music and Lyrics by GEORGE GERSHWIN,
DuBOSE and DOROTHY HEYWARD
and IRA GERSHWIN

THE LADY IS A TRAMP

from BABES IN ARMS

HORN

Words by LORENZ HART
Music by RICHARD RODGERS

Moderately bright

THE LAST NIGHT OF THE WORLD

from MISS SAIGON

Horn

Music by CLAUDE-MICHEL SCHÖNBERG
Lyrics by RICHARD MALTBY JR. and ALAIN BOUBLIL
Adapted from original French Lyrics by ALAIN BOUBLIL

LET'S CALL THE WHOLE THING OFF

from SHALL WE DANCE

Horn

Music and Lyrics by GEORGE GERSHWIN
and IRA GERSHWIN

LOVE IS HERE TO STAY
from GOLDWYN FOLLIES

Horn

Music and Lyrics by GEORGE GERSHWIN
and IRA GERSHWIN

LOVE ME OR LEAVE ME

from WHOOPEE!

HORN

Lyrics by GUS KAHN
Music by WALTER DONALDSON

LOVE WALKED IN

from GOLDWYN FOLLIES

Horn

Music and Lyrics by GEORGE GERSHWIN
and IRA GERSHWIN

LUCK BE A LADY
from GUYS AND DOLLS

Horn

By FRANK LOESSER

MAKIN' WHOOPEE!

from WHOOPEE!

Horn

Lyrics by GUS KAHN
Music by WALTER DONALDSON

MAME
from MAME

Horn

Music and Lyric by
JERRY HERMAN

MAMMA MIA
from MAMMA MIA!

Horn

Words and Music by BENNY ANDERSSON,
BJÖRN ULVAEUS and STIG ANDERSON

Moderately bright

MATCHMAKER
from the Musical FIDDLER ON THE ROOF

Words by SHELDON HARNICK
Music by JERRY BOCK

Horn

MAYBE

from the Musical Production ANNIE

Horn

Lyric by MARTIN CHARNIN
Music by CHARLES STROUSE

MEMORY

from CATS

Horn

Music by ANDREW LLOYD WEBBER
Text by TREVOR NUNN after T.S. ELIOT

THE MUSIC OF THE NIGHT

from THE PHANTOM OF THE OPERA

HORN

Music by ANDREW LLOYD WEBBER
Lyrics by CHARLES HART
Additional Lyrics by RICHARD STILGOE

Moderately slow

MY FAVORITE THINGS
from THE SOUND OF MUSIC

HORN

Lyrics by OSCAR HAMMERSTEIN II
Music by RICHARD RODGERS

Lively, with spirit

NICE WORK IF YOU CAN GET IT

from A DAMSEL IN DISTRESS

Horn

Music and Lyrics by GEORGE GERSHWIN
and IRA GERSWIN

OH, WHAT A BEAUTIFUL MORNIN'

from OKLAHOMA!

HORN

Lyrics by OSCAR HAMMERSTEIN II
Music by RICHARD RODGERS

Bright Waltz

OKLAHOMA

from OKLAHOMA!

HORN

Lyrics by OSCAR HAMMERSTEIN II
Music by RICHARD RODGERS

OL' MAN RIVER

from SHOW BOAT

HORN

Lyrics by OSCAR HAMMERSTEIN II
Music by JEROME KERN

OLD DEVIL MOON
from FINIAN'S RAINBOW

Horn

Words by E.Y. "YIP" HARBURG
Music by BURTON LANE

ON MY OWN
from LES MISÉRABLES

Music by CLAUDE-MICHEL SCHÖNBERG
Lyrics by ALAIN BOUBLIL, JEAN-MARC NATEL,
HERBERT KRETZMER, JOHN CAIRD
and TREVOR NUNN

Horn

ONCE IN A LIFETIME

from the Musical Production STOP THE WORLD—I WANT TO GET OFF

Horn

Words and Music by LESLIE BRICUSSE
and ANTHONY NEWLEY

ONCE IN LOVE WITH AMY
from WHERE'S CHARLEY?

HORN

By FRANK LOESSER

ONE
from A CHORUS LINE

Horn

Music by MARVIN HAMLISCH
Lyric by EDWARD KLEBAN

PEOPLE WILL SAY WE'RE IN LOVE

from OKLAHOMA!

HORN

Lyrics by OSCAR HAMMERSTEIN II
Music by RICHARD RODGERS

Moderately

THE PHANTOM OF THE OPERA
from THE PHANTOM OF THE OPERA

Horn

Music by ANDREW LLOYD WEBBER
Lyrics by CHARLES HART
Additional Lyrics by RICHARD STILGOE
and MIKE BATT

POPULAR
from the Broadway Musical WICKED

HORN

Music and Lyrics by
STEPHEN SCHWARTZ

73

SEASONS OF LOVE

from RENT

Horn

Words and Music by
JONATHAN LARSON

Moderately

SEND IN THE CLOWNS

from the Musical A LITTLE NIGHT MUSIC

Horn

Words and Music by
STEPHEN SONDHEIM

Slowly

SEVENTY SIX TROMBONES

from Meredith Willson's THE MUSIC MAN

Horn

By MEREDITH WILLSON

SHALL WE DANCE?

from THE KING AND I

Horn

Lyrics by OSCAR HAMMERSTEIN II
Music by RICHARD RODGERS

SHE LOVES ME

from SHE LOVES ME

Horn

Words by SHELDON HARNICK
Music by JERRY BOCK

SHERRY
featured in JERSEY BOYS

Horn

Words and Music by
BOB GAUDIO

SOME ENCHANTED EVENING

from SOUTH PACIFIC

Horn

Lyrics by OSCAR HAMMERSTEIN II
Music by RICHARD RODGERS

SUMMERTIME

from PORGY AND BESS®

Horn

Music and Lyrics by GEORGE GERSHWIN,
DuBOSE and DOROTHY HEYWARD
and IRA GERSHWIN

SUNRISE, SUNSET

from the Musical FIDDLER ON THE ROOF

Horn

Words by SHELDON HARNICK
Music by JERRY BOCK

SUPERSTAR

from JESUS CHRIST SUPERSTAR

Horn

Words by TIM RICE
Music by ANDREW LLOYD WEBBER

THE SURREY WITH THE FRINGE ON TOP

from OKLAHOMA!

HORN

Lyrics by OSCAR HAMMERSTEIN II
Music by RICHARD RODGERS

THE SWEETEST SOUNDS
from NO STRINGS

Horn

Lyrics and Music by
RICHARD RODGERS

Moderately

THERE'S NO BUSINESS LIKE SHOW BUSINESS

from the Stage Production ANNIE GET YOUR GUN

HORN

Words and Music by
IRVING BERLIN

THEY ALL LAUGHED

from SHALL WE DANCE

Horn

Music and Lyrics by GEORGE GERSHWIN
and IRA GERSHWIN

THEY CAN'T TAKE THAT AWAY FROM ME

from SHALL WE DANCE

Horn

Music and Lyrics by GEORGE GERSHWIN
and IRA GERSHWIN

THINK OF ME
from THE PHANTOM OF THE OPERA

Horn

Music by ANDREW LLOYD WEBBER
Lyrics by CHARLES HART
Additional Lyrics by RICHARD STILGOE

THIS IS THE MOMENT

from JEKYLL & HYDE

Horn

Words and Music by LESLIE BRICUSSE
and FRANK WILDHORN

THIS NEARLY WAS MINE

from SOUTH PACIFIC

HORN

Lyrics by OSCAR HAMMERSTEIN II
Music by RICHARD RODGERS

TILL THERE WAS YOU

from Meredith Willson's THE MUSIC MAN

Horn

By MEREDITH WILLSON

TOMORROW

from the Musical Production ANNIE

Horn

Lyric by MARTIN CHARNIN
Music by CHARLES STROUSE

WALK LIKE A MAN

featured in JERSEY BOYS

Horn

Words and Music by BOB CREWE
and BOB GAUDIO

UNUSUAL WAY

from NINE

Horn

Music and Lyrics by
MAURY YESTON

WHAT I DID FOR LOVE

from A CHORUS LINE

Horn

Music by MARVIN HAMLISCH
Lyric by EDWARD KLEBAN

Slowly

WHAT KIND OF FOOL AM I?

from the Musical Production STOP THE WORLD—I WANT TO GET OFF

Horn

Words and Music by LESLIE BRICUSSE
and ANTHONY NEWLEY

WHERE IS LOVE?

from the Broadway Musical OLIVER!

Horn

Words and Music by
LIONEL BART

WHO CAN I TURN TO
(When Nobody Needs Me)
from THE ROAR OF THE GREASEPAINT—THE SMELL OF THE CROWD

Words and Music by LESLIE BRICUSSE
and ANTHONY NEWLEY

Horn

Slowly

A WHOLE NEW WORLD

from the Walt Disney Stageplay ALADDIN

HORN

Music by ALAN MENKEN
Lyrics by TIM RICE

WILL YOU LOVE ME TOMORROW
(Will You Still Love Me Tomorrow)
from BEAUTIFUL

Horn

Words and Music by GERRY GOFFIN
and CAROLE KING

WITH ONE LOOK

from SUNSET BOULEVARD

HORN

Music by ANDREW LLOYD WEBBER
Lyrics by DON BLACK and CHRISTOPHER HAMPTON,
with contributions by AMY POWERS

WRITTEN IN THE STARS

from Elton John and Tim Rice's AIDA

HORN

Music by ELTON JOHN
Lyrics by TIM RICE

YOU RULE MY WORLD

from THE FULL MONTY

Horn

Words and Music by
DAVID YAZBEK

YOU'LL NEVER WALK ALONE
from CAROUSEL

HORN

Lyrics by OSCAR HAMMERSTEIN II
Music by RICHARD RODGERS

YOU'LL BE IN MY HEART

Disney Presents TARZAN The Broadway Musical

HORN

Words and Music by
PHIL COLLINS

D.S. al Coda

YOU'VE GOT A FRIEND

from BEAUTIFUL

Horn

Words and Music by
CAROLE KING

Moderately

YOUNGER THAN SPRINGTIME
from SOUTH PACIFIC

Horn

Lyrics by OSCAR HAMMERSTEIN II
Music by RICHARD RODGERS